**To:**

_____

**From:**

_____

*Do not merely listen to the Word,*
*and so deceive yourselves.*
*Do what it says.*

(N.I.V)

*James 1:22*

GODSTRONG

My Sunday Journal™ by Godstrong™
© 2005 by Godstrong, Inc.
ISBN 0-9772583-0-0

Requests for information should be e-mailed to info@Godstrong.org.

Project Managers: Collin Endress & Aaron Carnahan
Editor: Robin Halsey
Introduction: Paul I. Harshbarger
Design: Garrett Rittenberry, Guerrilla Design (www.guerilladesign.com)
Printed in China.

# *My Sunday Journal* ™

BY

# GODSTRONG ™

# My Sunday Journal by GODSTRONG

*My Sunday Journal* by GODSTRONG is your solution to organizing and referencing your Sunday sermon notes. It is a tool to help you structure your Sunday note taking and to remind you of what God has revealed to you. As you meditate on scripture and your sermon notes, allow God to penetrate your heart. God longs to become more and more real in each of our lives, and one way He can do that is by teaching us through the proclamation of His truth.

God is faithful to teach us from His Word and transform us into the people He longs for us to be. James 1:22 tells us, **"Do not merely listen to the word, and so deceive yourselves. Do what it says."** (New International Version) So how will you remember what God wants you to do? By recording what you've learned from God's Word, you are able to retain and reflect upon those Biblical truths.

That is the whole purpose of *My Sunday Journal*. It provides a place for you to write down what God is saying to you. Each entry becomes a resource that can be used again and again to recall the truths that God has taught you. Each week you can customize your easy Reference Index with the journal page number, sermon topic, key verse, speaker and date. The Reference Index allows you to quickly locate information you wish to recall. Reviewing your notes helps you to apply God's Word to your life.

When your pastor or teacher says something that you want to remember, write it down! When a verse is referred to but you don't have time to look it up, mark it down! When God gives you an insight into your spiritual life, put it in writing. When a new truth from God's Word strikes you, jot it down so you can meditate on it later.

So grab your Bible, a pen, and *My Sunday Journal* and get started. Class is in session and the Bible is the subject. Take good notes and allow the transforming power of God to mold you into the person He wants you to be.

**GODSTRONG**

# Reference Index

*Fill in the blanks after each Sunday Sermon for quick and easy reference. The first row has been filled out for you as an example.

| Page | Topic | Key Verse/ Chapter | Speaker | Date |
|------|-------|--------------------|---------|------|
| 0 | Salvation | John 3:16 | John Q. Speaker | 01/01/01 |

# Reference Index

Revelation

( 1: 20 ) The meaning of the seven stars,
you saw in my right hand, and the
seven golden candlesticks:
   The seven ~~churches~~ stars are the
leaders of the seven churches, and
the seven candlesticks are the
churches themselfes.

*Psalm 119:2*

*Blessed are they that keep his testimonies, and that seek him with the whole heart.*

Date: _____

Topic: _____

Key Chapter/Verse: _____

Speaker: _____

Notes: _____

_____

_____

_____

_____

_____

_____

_____

_____

_____

_____

_____

_____

_____

_____

_____

_____

_____

_____

_____

_____

_____

_____

_____

_____

_____

_____

_____

_____

Notes:
_____
_____
_____
_____
_____
_____
_____
_____
_____
_____
_____
_____
_____
_____
_____
_____
_____
_____
_____

Reference Verses:
_____
_____
_____
_____
_____
_____

### Application / Reflection
"How will I use this message to change my life for Christ?"
_____
_____
_____
_____
_____

*Psalm 119:9*

*Wherewithal shall a young man cleanse his way? by taking heed thereto according to thy word.*

Date: _____

Topic: _____

Key Chapter/Verse: _____

Speaker: _____

Notes: _____
_____
_____
_____
_____
_____
_____
_____
_____
_____
_____
_____
_____
_____
_____
_____
_____
_____
_____
_____
_____
_____
_____
_____
_____
_____
_____
_____
_____

Notes:

_____
_____
_____
_____
_____
_____
_____
_____
_____
_____
_____
_____
_____
_____
_____
_____
_____
_____

Reference Verses:

_____
_____
_____
_____
_____

## Application / Reflection
"How will I use this message to change my life for Christ?"

_____
_____
_____
_____

*Psalm 119 :11*
*Thy word have I hid in mine heart, that I might not sin against thee.*

Date: _____

Topic: _____

Key Chapter/Verse: _____

Speaker: _____

Notes: _____
_____
_____
_____
_____
_____
_____
_____
_____
_____
_____
_____
_____
_____
_____
_____
_____
_____
_____
_____
_____
_____
_____
_____
_____
_____
_____

Notes:

_____
_____
_____
_____
_____
_____
_____
_____
_____
_____
_____
_____
_____
_____
_____
_____
_____
_____
_____
_____

Reference Verses:

_____
_____
_____
_____
_____

### Application / Reflection
"How will I use this message to change my life for Christ?"
_____
_____
_____
_____

*Psalm 119:12*

*Blessed art thou, O LORD: teach me thy statutes.*

Date: _____

Topic: _____

Key Chapter/Verse: _____

Speaker: _____

Notes: _____

_____

_____

_____

_____

_____

_____

_____

_____

_____

_____

_____

_____

_____

_____

_____

_____

_____

_____

_____

_____

_____

_____

_____

_____

_____

Notes:

_____
_____
_____
_____
_____
_____
_____
_____
_____
_____
_____
_____
_____
_____
_____
_____
_____
_____
_____

Reference Verses:

_____
_____
_____
_____
_____

## Application / Reflection

"How will I use this message to change my life for Christ?"

_____
_____
_____
_____
_____

*Psalm 119:15*

*I will meditate in thy precepts, and have respect unto thy ways.*

Date: _____

Topic: _____

Key Chapter/Verse: _____

Speaker: _____

Notes: _____

_____

_____

_____

_____

_____

_____

_____

_____

_____

_____

_____

_____

_____

_____

_____

_____

_____

_____

_____

_____

_____

_____

_____

_____

_____

_____

_____

_____

Notes:

_____
_____
_____
_____
_____
_____
_____
_____
_____
_____
_____
_____
_____
_____
_____
_____
_____
_____
_____
_____

Reference Verses:

_____
_____
_____
_____
_____

### Application / Reflection
"How will I use this message to change my life for Christ?"

_____
_____
_____
_____
_____

*I I Timothy 3:16-17 All scripture is given by inspiration of God, and is profitable for doctrine, for reproof, for correction, for instruction in righteousness:  17 That the man of God may be perfect, thoroughly furnished unto all good works.*

Date: _____

Topic: _____

Key Chapter/Verse: _____

Speaker: _____

Notes: _____
_____
_____
_____
_____
_____
_____
_____
_____
_____
_____
_____
_____
_____
_____
_____
_____
_____
_____
_____
_____
_____
_____
_____
_____
_____
_____
_____
_____

Notes:

_____
_____
_____
_____
_____
_____
_____
_____
_____
_____
_____
_____
_____
_____
_____
_____
_____
_____

Reference Verses:

_____
_____
_____
_____
_____

## Application / Reflection
"How will I use this message to change my life for Christ?"

_____
_____
_____
_____
_____

*Psalm 119:16*

*I will delight myself in thy statutes: I will not forget thy word.*

Date: _____

Topic: _____

Key Chapter/Verse: _____

Speaker: _____

Notes: _____

_____

_____

_____

_____

_____

_____

_____

_____

_____

_____

_____

_____

_____

_____

_____

_____

_____

_____

_____

_____

_____

_____

_____

_____

_____

_____

_____

Notes:
_____
_____
_____
_____
_____
_____
_____
_____
_____
_____
_____
_____
_____
_____
_____
_____
_____
_____
_____

Reference Verses:
_____
_____
_____
_____
_____

**Application / Reflection**
"How will I use this message to change my life for Christ?"
_____
_____
_____
_____

*Psalm 119:24*
*Thy testimonies also are my delight and my counselors.*

Date: _____

Topic: _____

Key Chapter/Verse: _____

Speaker: _____

Notes: _____
_____
_____
_____
_____
_____
_____
_____
_____
_____
_____
_____
_____
_____
_____
_____
_____
_____
_____
_____
_____
_____
_____
_____
_____
_____
_____
_____
_____

Notes:

_____
_____
_____
_____
_____
_____
_____
_____
_____
_____
_____
_____
_____
_____
_____
_____
_____
_____
_____
_____
_____

Reference Verses:

_____
_____
_____
_____
_____

## Application / Reflection
"How will I use this message to change my life for Christ?"

_____
_____
_____
_____

*Psalm 119:27*

*Make me to understand the way of thy precepts: so shall I talk of thy wondrous works.*

Date: _____

Topic: _____

Key Chapter/Verse: _____

Speaker: _____

Notes: _____

_____

_____

_____

_____

_____

_____

_____

_____

_____

_____

_____

_____

_____

_____

_____

_____

_____

_____

_____

_____

_____

_____

_____

_____

_____

_____

_____

Notes:
_____
_____
_____
_____
_____
_____
_____
_____
_____
_____
_____
_____
_____
_____
_____
_____
_____
_____
_____

Reference Verses:
_____
_____
_____
_____
_____
_____

### Application / Reflection
"How will I use this message to change my life for Christ?"
_____
_____
_____
_____
_____

*Psalm 119:28*

*My soul melteth for heaviness: strengthen thou me according unto thy word.*

Date: _____

Topic: _____

Key Chapter/Verse: _____

Speaker: _____

Notes: _____
_____
_____
_____
_____
_____
_____
_____
_____
_____
_____
_____
_____
_____
_____
_____
_____
_____
_____
_____
_____
_____
_____
_____
_____
_____
_____
_____

Notes:
_____
_____
_____
_____
_____
_____
_____
_____
_____
_____
_____
_____
_____
_____
_____
_____
_____
_____
_____

Reference Verses:
_____
_____
_____
_____
_____

### Application / Reflection
"How will I use this message to change my life for Christ?"
_____
_____
_____
_____

*Psalm 119:31*

*I have stuck unto thy testimonies: O LORD, put me not to shame.*

Date: _____

Topic: _____

Key Chapter/Verse: _____

Speaker: _____

Notes: _____

_____
_____
_____
_____
_____
_____
_____
_____
_____
_____
_____
_____
_____
_____
_____
_____
_____
_____
_____
_____
_____
_____
_____
_____
_____
_____
_____
_____

Notes:
_____
_____
_____
_____
_____
_____
_____
_____
_____
_____
_____
_____
_____
_____
_____
_____
_____
_____

Reference Verses:
_____
_____
_____
_____
_____

## Application / Reflection
"How will I use this message to change my life for Christ?"
_____
_____
_____
_____
_____

*Psalm 119:32*
*I will run the way of thy commandments, when thou shalt enlarge my heart.*

Date: _____

Topic: _____

Key Chapter/Verse: _____

Speaker: _____

Notes: _____

_____
_____
_____
_____
_____
_____
_____
_____
_____
_____
_____
_____
_____
_____
_____
_____
_____
_____
_____
_____
_____
_____
_____
_____
_____
_____

Notes:

_____
_____
_____
_____
_____
_____
_____
_____
_____
_____
_____
_____
_____
_____
_____
_____
_____
_____
_____

Reference Verses:

_____
_____
_____
_____
_____

### Application / Reflection
"How will I use this message to change my life for Christ?"

_____
_____
_____
_____
_____

*Heb 4:12  For the word of God is quick, and powerful, and sharper than any twoedged sword, piercing even to the dividing asunder of soul and spirit, and of the joints and marrow, and is a discerner of the thoughts and intents of the heart.*

Date: _____

Topic: _____

Key Chapter/Verse: _____

Speaker: _____

Notes: _____
_____
_____
_____
_____
_____
_____
_____
_____
_____
_____
_____
_____
_____
_____
_____
_____
_____
_____
_____
_____
_____
_____
_____
_____
_____

Notes:

_____

_____

_____

_____

_____

_____

_____

_____

_____

_____

_____

_____

_____

_____

_____

_____

_____

_____

Reference Verses:

_____

_____

_____

_____

_____

### Application / Reflection
"How will I use this message to change my life for Christ?"

_____

_____

_____

_____

*Psalm 119:33*

*Teach me, O LORD, the way of thy statutes; and I shall keep it unto the end.*

Date: _____

Topic: _____

Key Chapter/Verse: _____

Speaker: _____

Notes: _____

_____

_____

_____

_____

_____

_____

_____

_____

_____

_____

_____

_____

_____

_____

_____

_____

_____

_____

_____

_____

_____

_____

_____

_____

_____

_____

_____

Notes:

_____
_____
_____
_____
_____
_____
_____
_____
_____
_____
_____
_____
_____
_____
_____
_____
_____
_____
_____
_____

Reference Verses:

_____
_____
_____
_____
_____

### Application / Reflection
"How will I use this message to change my life for Christ?"

_____
_____
_____
_____
_____

*Psalm 119:35*

*Make me to go in the path of thy commandments; for therein do I delight.*

Date: _____

Topic: _____

Key Chapter/Verse: _____

Speaker: _____

Notes: _____

_____

_____

_____

_____

_____

_____

_____

_____

_____

_____

_____

_____

_____

_____

_____

_____

_____

_____

_____

_____

_____

_____

_____

_____

_____

Notes:

_____
_____
_____
_____
_____
_____
_____
_____
_____
_____
_____
_____
_____
_____
_____
_____
_____
_____
_____
_____

Reference Verses:

_____
_____
_____
_____
_____

### Application / Reflection
"How will I use this message to change my life for Christ?"

_____
_____
_____
_____
_____

*Psalm 119:48*

*My hands also will I lift up unto thy commandments,*
*which I have loved; and I will meditate in thy statutes.*

Date: _____

Topic: _____

Key Chapter/Verse: _____

Speaker: _____

Notes: _____
_____
_____
_____
_____
_____
_____
_____
_____
_____
_____
_____
_____
_____
_____
_____
_____
_____
_____
_____
_____
_____
_____
_____
_____
_____
_____

Notes:

_____

_____

_____

_____

_____

_____

_____

_____

_____

_____

_____

_____

_____

_____

_____

_____

_____

_____

Reference Verses:

_____

_____

_____

_____

_____

### Application / Reflection
"How will I use this message to change my life for Christ?"

_____

_____

_____

_____

_____

*Psalm 119:54*
*Thy statutes have been my songs in the house of my pilgrimage.*

Date: _____

Topic: _____

Key Chapter/Verse: _____

Speaker: _____

Notes: _____
_____
_____
_____
_____
_____
_____
_____
_____
_____
_____
_____
_____
_____
_____
_____
_____
_____
_____
_____
_____
_____
_____
_____
_____
_____
_____
_____

Notes:

_____

_____

_____

_____

_____

_____

_____

_____

_____

_____

_____

_____

_____

_____

_____

_____

_____

_____

_____

_____

Reference Verses:

_____

_____

_____

_____

_____

_____

### Application / Reflection
"How will I use this message to change my life for Christ?"

_____

_____

_____

_____

*Psalm 119:66*

*Teach me good judgment and knowledge: for I have believed thy commandments.*

Date: _____

Topic: _____

Key Chapter/Verse: _____

Speaker: _____

Notes: _____

_____

_____

_____

_____

_____

_____

_____

_____

_____

_____

_____

_____

_____

_____

_____

_____

_____

_____

_____

_____

_____

_____

_____

_____

_____

_____

_____

_____

Notes:

_____
_____
_____
_____
_____
_____
_____
_____
_____
_____
_____
_____
_____
_____
_____
_____
_____
_____
_____

Reference Verses:

_____
_____
_____
_____
_____

## Application / Reflection
"How will I use this message to change my life for Christ?"

_____
_____
_____
_____
_____

*Psalm 119:68*

*Thou art good, and doest good; teach me thy statutes.*

Date: _____

Topic: _____

Key Chapter/Verse: _____

Speaker: _____

Notes: _____
_____
_____
_____
_____
_____
_____
_____
_____
_____
_____
_____
_____
_____
_____
_____
_____
_____
_____
_____
_____
_____
_____
_____
_____
_____
_____

Notes:

_____

_____

_____

_____

_____

_____

_____

_____

_____

_____

_____

_____

_____

_____

_____

_____

_____

Reference Verses:

_____

_____

_____

_____

_____

### Application / Reflection

"How will I use this message to change my life for Christ?"

_____

_____

_____

_____

*Psalm 43:10*

*Teach me to do thy will; for thou art my God: thy spirit is good; lead me into the land of uprightness.*

Date: _____

Topic: _____

Key Chapter/Verse: _____

Speaker: _____

Notes: _____

_____
_____
_____
_____
_____
_____
_____
_____
_____
_____
_____
_____
_____
_____
_____
_____
_____
_____
_____
_____
_____
_____
_____
_____
_____
_____
_____
_____
_____

Notes:

_____

_____

_____

_____

_____

_____

_____

_____

_____

_____

_____

_____

_____

_____

_____

_____

_____

_____

Reference Verses:

_____

_____

_____

_____

## Application / Reflection
"How will I use this message to change my life for Christ?"

_____

_____

_____

_____

_____

*Psalm 119:73*

*Thy hands have made me and fashioned me: give me under-standing, that I may learn thy commandments.*

Date: _____

Topic: _____

Key Chapter/Verse: _____

Speaker: _____

Notes: _____

_____

_____

_____

_____

_____

_____

_____

_____

_____

_____

_____

_____

_____

_____

_____

_____

_____

_____

_____

_____

_____

_____

_____

_____

_____

_____

_____

_____

Notes:

_____
_____
_____
_____
_____
_____
_____
_____
_____
_____
_____
_____
_____
_____
_____
_____
_____
_____
_____

Reference Verses:

_____
_____
_____
_____
_____
_____

### Application / Reflection
"How will I use this message to change my life for Christ?"

_____
_____
_____
_____

*Psalm 119:81*

*My soul fainteth for thy salvation: but I hope in thy word.*

Date: _____

Topic: _____

Key Chapter/Verse: _____

Speaker: _____

Notes: _____

_____

_____

_____

_____

_____

_____

_____

_____

_____

_____

_____

_____

_____

_____

_____

_____

_____

_____

_____

_____

_____

_____

_____

_____

_____

_____

_____

_____

Notes:
_____
_____
_____
_____
_____
_____
_____
_____
_____
_____
_____
_____
_____
_____
_____
_____
_____
_____

Reference Verses:
_____
_____
_____
_____
_____

**Application / Reflection**
"How will I use this message to change my life for Christ?"
_____
_____
_____
_____
_____

*Psalm 119:86*

*All your commands are trustworthy; help me, for men persecute me without cause. NIV*

Date: _____

Topic: _____

Key Chapter/Verse: _____

Speaker: _____

Notes: _____
_____
_____
_____
_____
_____
_____
_____
_____
_____
_____
_____
_____
_____
_____
_____
_____
_____
_____
_____
_____
_____
_____
_____
_____
_____
_____
_____
_____
_____
_____

Notes:

_____
_____
_____
_____
_____
_____
_____
_____
_____
_____
_____
_____
_____
_____
_____
_____
_____
_____

Reference Verses:

_____
_____
_____
_____
_____

## Application / Reflection
"How will I use this message to change my life for Christ?"

_____
_____
_____
_____

*Psalm 119:89*

*For ever, O LORD, thy word is settled in heaven.*

Date: _____

Topic: _____

Key Chapter/Verse: _____

Speaker: _____

Notes: _____

_____

_____

_____

_____

_____

_____

_____

_____

_____

_____

_____

_____

_____

_____

_____

_____

_____

_____

_____

_____

_____

_____

_____

_____

_____

_____

_____

_____

_____

Notes:
_____
_____
_____
_____
_____
_____
_____
_____
_____
_____
_____
_____
_____
_____
_____
_____
_____
_____

Reference Verses:
_____
_____
_____
_____
_____

### Application / Reflection
"How will I use this message to change my life for Christ?"
_____
_____
_____
_____
_____

*Psalm 119:93*

*I will never forget thy precepts: for with them thou hast quickened me.*

Date: _____

Topic: _____

Key Chapter/Verse: _____

Speaker: _____

Notes: _____

_____

_____

_____

_____

_____

_____

_____

_____

_____

_____

_____

_____

_____

_____

_____

_____

_____

_____

_____

_____

_____

_____

_____

_____

_____

Notes:

_____
_____
_____
_____
_____
_____
_____
_____
_____
_____
_____
_____
_____
_____
_____
_____
_____
_____

Reference Verses:

_____
_____
_____
_____
_____

## Application / Reflection
"How will I use this message to change my life for Christ?"

_____
_____
_____
_____
_____

*Psalm 119:98*
*Thou through thy commandments hast made me wiser than mine enemies: for they are ever with me.*

Date: _____

Topic: _____

Key Chapter/Verse: _____

Speaker: _____

Notes: _____

_____
_____
_____
_____
_____
_____
_____
_____
_____
_____
_____
_____
_____
_____
_____
_____
_____
_____
_____
_____
_____
_____
_____
_____
_____
_____
_____

Notes:

_____
_____
_____
_____
_____
_____
_____
_____
_____
_____
_____
_____
_____
_____
_____
_____
_____
_____
_____

Reference Verses:

_____
_____
_____
_____
_____

### Application / Reflection
"How will I use this message to change my life for Christ?"

_____
_____
_____
_____

*James 1:22*

*But be ye doers of the word, and not hearers only, deceiving your own selves.*

Date: _____

Topic: _____

Key Chapter/Verse: _____

Speaker: _____

Notes: _____

_____

_____

_____

_____

_____

_____

_____

_____

_____

_____

_____

_____

_____

_____

_____

_____

_____

_____

_____

_____

_____

_____

_____

_____

_____

_____

_____

_____

Notes:
_____
_____
_____
_____
_____
_____
_____
_____
_____
_____
_____
_____
_____
_____
_____
_____
_____
_____
_____
_____

Reference Verses:
_____
_____
_____
_____
_____

### Application / Reflection
"How will I use this message to change my life for Christ?"
_____
_____
_____
_____
_____

*Psalm 119:103*

*How sweet are thy words unto my taste! yea, sweeter than honey to my mouth!*

Date: _____

Topic: _____

Key Chapter/Verse: _____

Speaker: _____

Notes: _____

_____

_____

_____

_____

_____

_____

_____

_____

_____

_____

_____

_____

_____

_____

_____

_____

_____

_____

_____

_____

_____

_____

_____

_____

_____

Notes:

_____
_____
_____
_____
_____
_____
_____
_____
_____
_____
_____
_____
_____
_____
_____
_____
_____
_____
_____

Reference Verses:

_____
_____
_____
_____
_____

### Application / Reflection
"How will I use this message to change my life for Christ?"

_____
_____
_____
_____
_____

*Psalm 119:104*

*Through thy precepts I get understanding: therefore I hate every false way.*

Date: _____

Topic: _____

Key Chapter/Verse: _____

Speaker: _____

Notes: _____

_____

_____

_____

_____

_____

_____

_____

_____

_____

_____

_____

_____

_____

_____

_____

_____

_____

_____

_____

_____

_____

_____

_____

_____

_____

_____

_____

_____

Notes:

_____

_____

_____

_____

_____

_____

_____

_____

_____

_____

_____

_____

_____

_____

_____

_____

_____

Reference Verses:

_____

_____

_____

_____

_____

_____

### Application / Reflection
"How will I use this message to change my life for Christ?"

_____

_____

_____

_____

*Psalm 119:105*

*Thy word is a lamp unto my feet, and a light unto my path.*

Date: _____

Topic: _____

Key Chapter/Verse: _____

Speaker: _____

Notes: _____

_____
_____
_____
_____
_____
_____
_____
_____
_____
_____
_____
_____
_____
_____
_____
_____
_____
_____
_____
_____
_____
_____
_____
_____
_____
_____
_____
_____
_____

Notes:

_____

_____

_____

_____

_____

_____

_____

_____

_____

_____

_____

_____

_____

_____

_____

_____

_____

_____

Reference Verses:

_____

_____

_____

_____

_____

### Application / Reflection
"How will I use this message to change my life for Christ?"

_____

_____

_____

_____

*Psalm 119:111*

*Thy testimonies have I taken as an heritage for ever: for they are the rejoicing of my heart.*

Date: _____

Topic: _____

Key Chapter/Verse: _____

Speaker: _____

Notes: _____

_____

_____

_____

_____

_____

_____

_____

_____

_____

_____

_____

_____

_____

_____

_____

_____

_____

_____

_____

_____

_____

_____

_____

_____

_____

_____

_____

## Notes:

_____
_____
_____
_____
_____
_____
_____
_____
_____
_____
_____
_____
_____
_____
_____
_____
_____
_____
_____

## Reference Verses:

_____
_____
_____
_____
_____
_____

### Application / Reflection
"How will I use this message to change my life for Christ?"

_____
_____
_____
_____

*Psalm 119:112*
*I have inclined mine heart to perform thy statutes alway,*
*even unto the end.*

Date: _____

Topic: _____

Key Chapter/Verse: _____

Speaker: _____

Notes: _____

_____

_____

_____

_____

_____

_____

_____

_____

_____

_____

_____

_____

_____

_____

_____

_____

_____

_____

_____

_____

_____

_____

_____

_____

_____

_____

Notes: _____

_____

_____

_____

_____

_____

_____

_____

_____

_____

_____

_____

_____

_____

_____

_____

_____

_____

_____

Reference Verses: _____

_____

_____

_____

_____

_____

### Application / Reflection
"How will I use this message to change my life for Christ?"

_____

_____

_____

_____

*Psalm 119:114*

*Thou art my hiding place and my shield: I hope in thy word.*

Date: _____

Topic: _____

Key Chapter/Verse: _____

Speaker: _____

Notes: _____

_____

_____

_____

_____

_____

_____

_____

_____

_____

_____

_____

_____

_____

_____

_____

_____

_____

_____

_____

_____

_____

_____

_____

_____

_____

_____

Notes:

_____

_____

_____

_____

_____

_____

_____

_____

_____

_____

_____

_____

_____

_____

_____

_____

_____

_____

Reference Verses:

_____

_____

_____

_____

_____

**Application / Reflection**

"How will I use this message to change my life for Christ?"

_____

_____

_____

_____

*James 1:23-24   For if any be a hearer of the word, and not a doer, he is like unto a man beholding his natural face in a glass: 24 For he beholdeth himself, and goeth his way, and straightway forgetteth what manner of man he was.*

Date:_____

Topic:_____

Key Chapter/Verse:_____

Speaker:_____

Notes:_____
_____
_____
_____
_____
_____
_____
_____
_____
_____
_____
_____
_____
_____
_____
_____
_____
_____
_____
_____
_____
_____
_____
_____
_____
_____
_____
_____
_____

Notes:

_____

_____

_____

_____

_____

_____

_____

_____

_____

_____

_____

_____

_____

_____

_____

_____

_____

Reference Verses:

_____

_____

_____

_____

_____

### Application / Reflection
"How will I use this message to change my life for Christ?"

_____

_____

_____

_____

*Psalm 119:125*

*I am thy servant; give me understanding, that I may know thy testimonies.*

Date: _____

Topic: _____

Key Chapter/Verse: _____

Speaker: _____

Notes: _____

_____

_____

_____

_____

_____

_____

_____

_____

_____

_____

_____

_____

_____

_____

_____

_____

_____

_____

_____

_____

_____

_____

_____

_____

_____

Notes:

_____

_____

_____

_____

_____

_____

_____

_____

_____

_____

_____

_____

_____

_____

_____

_____

_____

_____

Reference Verses:

_____

_____

_____

_____

_____

_____

### Application / Reflection
"How will I use this message to change my life for Christ?"

_____

_____

_____

_____

*Psalm 119:129*

*Thy testimonies are wonderful: therefore doth my soul keep them.*

Date: _____

Topic: _____

Key Chapter/Verse: _____

Speaker: _____

Notes: _____
_____
_____
_____
_____
_____
_____
_____
_____
_____
_____
_____
_____
_____
_____
_____
_____
_____
_____
_____
_____
_____
_____
_____
_____
_____
_____
_____
_____
_____
_____

Notes:

_____
_____
_____
_____
_____
_____
_____
_____
_____
_____
_____
_____
_____
_____
_____
_____
_____
_____

Reference Verses:

_____
_____
_____
_____
_____

## Application / Reflection
"How will I use this message to change my life for Christ?"

_____
_____
_____
_____
_____

*Psalm 119:130*
*The entrance of thy words giveth light; it giveth*
*understanding unto the simple.*

Date: _____

Topic: _____

Key Chapter/Verse: _____

Speaker: _____

Notes: _____
_____
_____
_____
_____
_____
_____
_____
_____
_____
_____
_____
_____
_____
_____
_____
_____
_____
_____
_____
_____
_____
_____
_____
_____
_____
_____
_____

Notes:
_____
_____
_____
_____
_____
_____
_____
_____
_____
_____
_____
_____
_____
_____
_____
_____
_____
_____
_____
_____

Reference Verses:
_____
_____
_____
_____
_____
_____

### Application / Reflection
"How will I use this message to change my life for Christ?"
_____
_____
_____
_____
_____

*Psalm 119 :133*

*Order my steps in thy word: and let not any iniquity have dominion over me.*

Date: _____

Topic: _____

Key Chapter/Verse: _____

Speaker: _____

Notes: _____

_____

_____

_____

_____

_____

_____

_____

_____

_____

_____

_____

_____

_____

_____

_____

_____

_____

_____

_____

_____

_____

_____

_____

_____

_____

_____

_____

_____

Notes:

_____

_____

_____

_____

_____

_____

_____

_____

_____

_____

_____

_____

_____

_____

_____

_____

_____

_____

Reference Verses:

_____

_____

_____

_____

_____

### Application / Reflection
"How will I use this message to change my life for Christ?"

_____

_____

_____

_____

_____

*Psalm 119:135*

*Make thy face to shine upon thy servant; and teach me thy statutes.*

Date: _____

Topic: _____

Key Chapter/Verse: _____

Speaker: _____

Notes: _____

_____

_____

_____

_____

_____

_____

_____

_____

_____

_____

_____

_____

_____

_____

_____

_____

_____

_____

_____

_____

_____

_____

_____

_____

_____

_____

_____

Notes:

_____
_____
_____
_____
_____
_____
_____
_____
_____
_____
_____
_____
_____
_____
_____
_____
_____
_____
_____

Reference Verses:

_____
_____
_____
_____
_____

## Application / Reflection
"How will I use this message to change my life for Christ?"

_____
_____
_____
_____
_____

*Psalm 119:138*

*Thy testimonies that thou hast commanded are righteous and very faithful.*

Date: _____

Topic: _____

Key Chapter/Verse: _____

Speaker: _____

Notes: _____
_____
_____
_____
_____
_____
_____
_____
_____
_____
_____
_____
_____
_____
_____
_____
_____
_____
_____
_____
_____
_____
_____
_____
_____
_____
_____
_____
_____

Notes:

_____
_____
_____
_____
_____
_____
_____
_____
_____
_____
_____
_____
_____
_____
_____
_____
_____
_____
_____

Reference Verses:

_____
_____
_____
_____
_____
_____

### Application / Reflection
"How will I use this message to change my life for Christ?"

_____
_____
_____
_____
_____

*Psalm 119:151*

*Thou art near, O LORD; and all thy commandments
are truth.*

Date: _____

Topic: _____

Key Chapter/Verse: _____

Speaker: _____

Notes: _____
_____
_____
_____
_____
_____
_____
_____
_____
_____
_____
_____
_____
_____
_____
_____
_____
_____
_____
_____
_____
_____
_____
_____
_____
_____
_____

Notes:
_____
_____
_____
_____
_____
_____
_____
_____
_____
_____
_____
_____
_____
_____
_____
_____
_____
_____

Reference Verses:
_____
_____
_____
_____
_____
_____

### Application / Reflection
"How will I use this message to change my life for Christ?"
_____
_____
_____
_____
_____

*Psalm 119:159*

*Consider how I love thy precepts: quicken me, O LORD, according to thy lovingkindness.*

Date: _____

Topic: _____

Key Chapter/Verse: _____

Speaker: _____

Notes: _____

_____

_____

_____

_____

_____

_____

_____

_____

_____

_____

_____

_____

_____

_____

_____

_____

_____

_____

_____

_____

_____

_____

_____

_____

_____

_____

_____

Notes:

_____
_____
_____
_____
_____
_____
_____
_____
_____
_____
_____
_____
_____
_____
_____
_____
_____

Reference Verses:

_____
_____
_____
_____
_____

### Application / Reflection
"How will I use this message to change my life for Christ?"

_____
_____
_____
_____
_____

*Romans 10: 17*

*So then faith cometh by hearing, and hearing by the word of God.*

Date: _____

Topic: _____

Key Chapter/Verse: _____

Speaker: _____

Notes: _____

_____

_____

_____

_____

_____

_____

_____

_____

_____

_____

_____

_____

_____

_____

_____

_____

_____

_____

_____

_____

_____

_____

_____

_____

_____

_____

Notes:

_____

_____

_____

_____

_____

_____

_____

_____

_____

_____

_____

_____

_____

_____

_____

_____

_____

_____

Reference Verses:

_____

_____

_____

_____

_____

_____

### Application / Reflection
"How will I use this message to change my life for Christ?"

_____

_____

_____

_____

*Psalm 119:166*
*LORD, I have hoped for thy salvation, and done thy commandments.*

Date: _____

Topic: _____

Key Chapter/Verse: _____

Speaker: _____

Notes: _____
_____
_____
_____
_____
_____
_____
_____
_____
_____
_____
_____
_____
_____
_____
_____
_____
_____
_____
_____
_____
_____
_____
_____
_____
_____
_____
_____

Notes:

_____
_____
_____
_____
_____
_____
_____
_____
_____
_____
_____
_____
_____
_____
_____
_____
_____

Reference Verses:

_____
_____
_____
_____
_____
_____

### Application / Reflection
"How will I use this message to change my life for Christ?"

_____
_____
_____
_____

*Psalm 119:167*
*My soul hath kept thy testimonies; and I love them exceedingly.*

Date: _____

Topic: _____

Key Chapter/Verse: _____

Speaker: _____

Notes: _____
_____
_____
_____
_____
_____
_____
_____
_____
_____
_____
_____
_____
_____
_____
_____
_____
_____
_____
_____
_____
_____
_____
_____
_____
_____
_____
_____
_____

Notes:

_____
_____
_____
_____
_____
_____
_____
_____
_____
_____
_____
_____
_____
_____
_____
_____
_____
_____
_____

Reference Verses:

_____
_____
_____
_____
_____

## Application / Reflection
"How will I use this message to change my life for Christ?"
_____
_____
_____
_____

*Psalm 119:168*

*I have kept thy precepts and thy testimonies: for all my ways are before thee.*

Date: _____

Topic: _____

Key Chapter/Verse: _____

Speaker: _____

Notes: _____

_____

_____

_____

_____

_____

_____

_____

_____

_____

_____

_____

_____

_____

_____

_____

_____

_____

_____

_____

_____

_____

_____

_____

_____

_____

_____

Notes:

_____
_____
_____
_____
_____
_____
_____
_____
_____
_____
_____
_____
_____
_____
_____
_____
_____
_____
_____
_____

Reference Verses:

_____
_____
_____
_____
_____
_____

### Application / Reflection
"How will I use this message to change my life for Christ?"

_____
_____
_____
_____

*Psalm 119:169*

*Let my cry come near before thee, O LORD: give me understanding according to thy word.*

Date: _____

Topic: _____

Key Chapter/Verse: _____

Speaker: _____

Notes: _____

_____

_____

_____

_____

_____

_____

_____

_____

_____

_____

_____

_____

_____

_____

_____

_____

_____

_____

_____

_____

_____

_____

_____

_____

_____

_____

Notes:

_____
_____
_____
_____
_____
_____
_____
_____
_____
_____
_____
_____
_____
_____
_____
_____
_____
_____
_____

Reference Verses:

_____
_____
_____
_____
_____

### Application / Reflection
"How will I use this message to change my life for Christ?"

_____
_____
_____
_____

*Psalm 119:171*

*My lips shall utter praise, when thou hast taught me thy statutes.*

Date: _____

Topic: _____

Key Chapter/Verse: _____

Speaker: _____

Notes: _____

_____
_____
_____
_____
_____
_____
_____
_____
_____
_____
_____
_____
_____
_____
_____
_____
_____
_____
_____
_____
_____
_____
_____
_____
_____
_____
_____
_____
_____

Notes:

_____
_____
_____
_____
_____
_____
_____
_____
_____
_____
_____
_____
_____
_____
_____
_____
_____
_____
_____

Reference Verses:

_____
_____
_____
_____
_____

## Application / Reflection
"How will I use this message to change my life for Christ?"

_____
_____
_____
_____
_____

*Psalm 119:172*

*My tongue shall speak of thy word: for all thy commandments are righteousness.*

Date: _____

Topic: _____

Key Chapter/Verse: _____

Speaker: _____

Notes: _____
_____
_____
_____
_____
_____
_____
_____
_____
_____
_____
_____
_____
_____
_____
_____
_____
_____
_____
_____
_____
_____
_____
_____
_____
_____
_____

Notes:

_____

_____

_____

_____

_____

_____

_____

_____

_____

_____

_____

_____

_____

_____

_____

_____

_____

_____

_____

Reference Verses:

_____

_____

_____

_____

_____

**Application / Reflection**

"How will I use this message to change my life for Christ?"

_____

_____

_____

_____

_____

*Psalm 119:173*

*Let thine hand help me; for I have chosen thy precepts.*

Date: _____

Topic: _____

Key Chapter/Verse: _____

Speaker: _____

Notes: _____
_____
_____
_____
_____
_____
_____
_____
_____
_____
_____
_____
_____
_____
_____
_____
_____
_____
_____
_____
_____
_____
_____
_____
_____
_____
_____
_____
_____
_____

Notes:

_____
_____
_____
_____
_____
_____
_____
_____
_____
_____
_____
_____
_____
_____
_____
_____
_____
_____
_____
_____

Reference Verses:

_____
_____
_____
_____
_____

### Application / Reflection
"How will I use this message to change my life for Christ?"

_____
_____
_____
_____

*Psalm 119:174*
*I have longed for thy salvation, O LORD; and thy law is my delight.*

Date: _____

Topic: _____

Key Chapter/Verse: _____

Speaker: _____

Notes: _____

_____

_____

_____

_____

_____

_____

_____

_____

_____

_____

_____

_____

_____

_____

_____

_____

_____

_____

_____

_____

_____

_____

_____

_____

_____

_____

Notes:

_____
_____
_____
_____
_____
_____
_____
_____
_____
_____
_____
_____
_____
_____
_____
_____
_____
_____
_____
_____

Reference Verses:

_____
_____
_____
_____
_____

### Application / Reflection
"How will I use this message to change my life for Christ?"

_____
_____
_____
_____
_____

John 1:14

And the Word was made flesh, and dwelt among us, (and we beheld his glory, the glory as of the only begotten of the Father,) full of grace and truth.

# Godstrong Mission

To boldly glorify Jesus Christ,
the source of our strength.

For more information regarding
Godstrong please visit our website
at www.godstrong.org.

E-mail: info@godstrong.org.

*God Bless and Be Godstrong!*

GODSTRONG